FIFTY NIFTY THINGS TO DO WITH A PAPER GROCERY BAG

Amusements, Disguises, Useful Items, Recipes, and More for Kids of All Ages!

By Denise Krebs

Illustrated by Brenda Beerhorst

Thank you to Katie, Marie, Meg and Kevin for having their nifty photos in this book.

FIFTY NIFTY THINGS TO DO WITH A PAPER GROCERY BAG

by Denise Krebs

illustrated by Brenda Beerhorst

Copyright © 1996

Educational Ministries, Inc.

ISBN 1-877871-92-3

Educational Ministries, Inc.

165 Plaza Drive

Prescott, AZ 86303-5549

800-221-0910

Printed on recycled paper.

A BIT OF HISTORY

The paper bags you will be using for these fifty nifty things are made on a machine that was patented by Charles Boughton Stilwell in 1883. His business was the Union Paper Bag Machine Company in Philadelphia. Mr. Stilwell's machine made the first square-bottom paper grocery bag. Before his invention, grocery bags were cone-shaped, often made from rolled newspaper, and didn't hold very many groceries. They were also harder to pack and wouldn't stand up. Mr. Stilwell's invention was very impor- tant to the grocery industry, and today twenty billion bags are made each year. Thank you, Mr. Stilwell, for your great invention. It's been more than 110 years, and paper bags are still useful and fun, too.

GETTING STARTED

Here is a bit of helpful information as you get started working on the projects in this book. Sometimes the bags will be used intact, just as they came from the store. But sometimes you will take the bag apart first. For some of the ideas, you will see a strange word of instruction: **TOT-BOB.** This stands for **Take Off the Bottom, Open Bag.** This can be done fairly easily by snipping off just the bot-

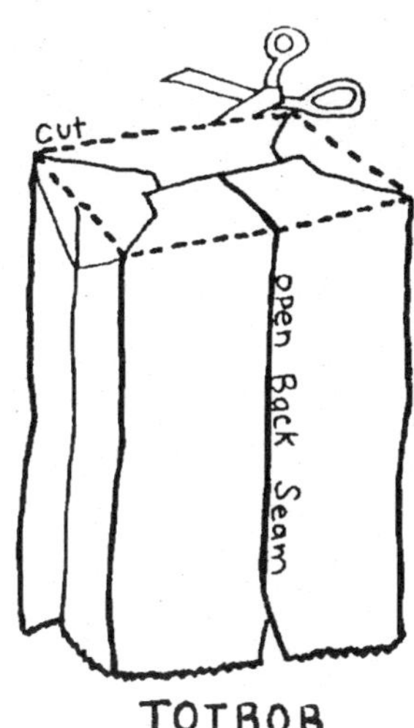

tom of the bag with scissors and then ripping the bag open along the back seam. When using a large grocery bag, you will end up with one large rectangle of paper, roughly seventeen inches by thirty-seven inches.

Remember, when you are finished making a project, you can recycle the scraps and goofs with your recyclable newspaper and cardboard.

1 BAT IT.

TOTBOB. Tightly roll up the large rectangle and tape it closed with masking tape. Crumple up the bottom of the bag into a rough ball. Wrap the ball with masking tape to make it round. This works great if you happen to forget to bring a bat and ball to a picnic!

2 BAKERY IT.

After baking bread, place the loaf in a paper bag to cool and transport.

3 BEAD IT.

TOTBOB. All the way down one long side of the paper make a mark at every inch. On the opposite side, beginning one-half inch from the end, do the same thing. Connect the marks with a pencil, making long, thin triangles. Cut them out. Starting with the wider side of the triangle begin rolling the paper tightly around a toothpick. After two or three turns, begin gluing the paper with white glue as you roll it all the way down to the point. Slide the bead off the toothpick, and allow it to dry. Paint the beads with acrylic paints, if you like. Spray on an acrylic sealer. String the beads onto a piece of yarn or embroidery floss. You can also make beads that are flat on the ends. Just cut one-inch rectangles instead of triangles. Then follow the same directions.

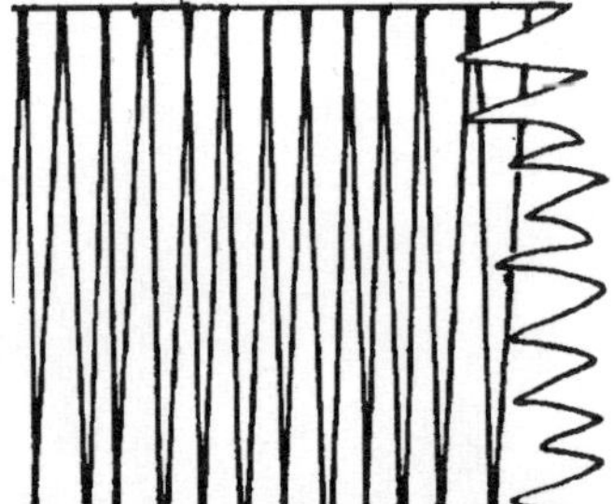

TOTBOB—Take off the bottom, open bag.

4 BEAR IT.

TOTBOB. Cut the large paper rectangle in half. You need just one half. Fold it into quarters. Draw the outline of 1/4 of a bear skin (as shown), and tear out the shape along the lines. Unfold it to see the bear-skin rug you've made. With a crayon or marker, draw native American symbols on the rug to tell a story. Crumple it up and smooth it out again to give it texture.

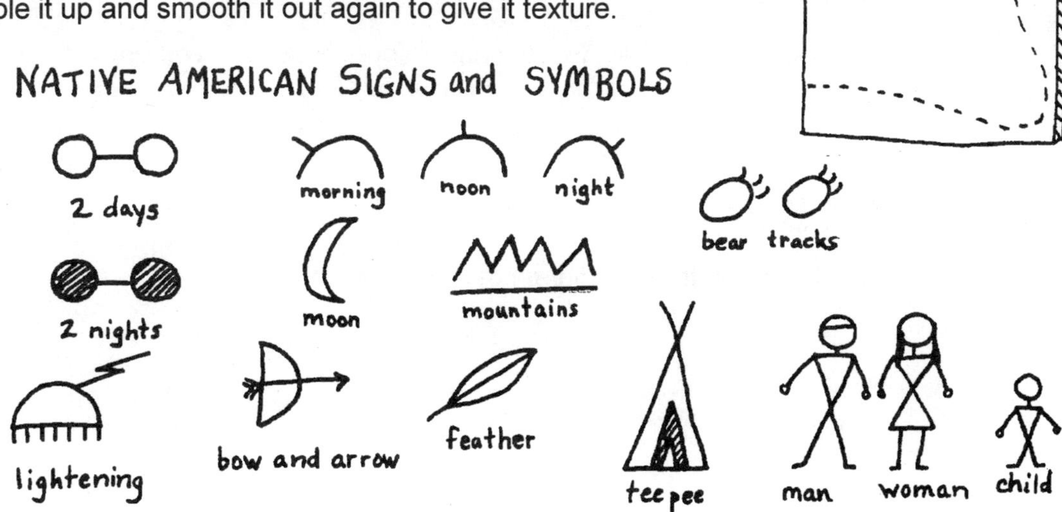

TOTBOB—Take off the bottom, open bag.

5 BLIND IT.

Put a bag over your head for a blindfold.

6 BLOW IT.

Try blowing up a paper bag, like a giant balloon. Now, can you pop it?

7 BOOK BAG IT.

Carry books to and from the library in a grocery bag.

8 BUTTERFLY IT.

TOTBOB. Cut out a huge butterfly shape from the large rectangle. Paint it. Mount the body and wings onto two crossed sticks. Fly it from the ceiling on a string, upside down so you can see the designs you painted.

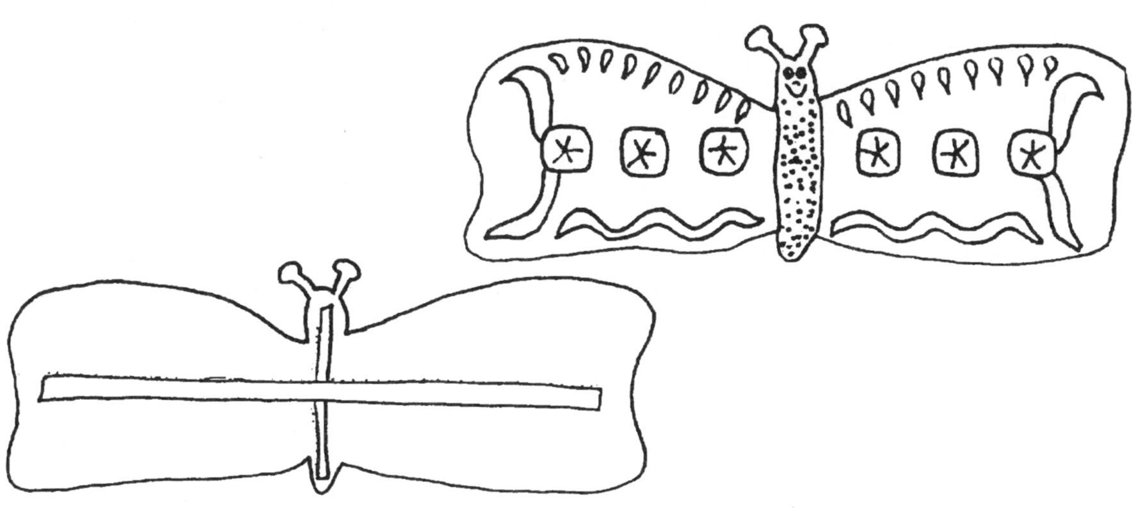

TOTBOB—Take off the bottom, open bag.

9 CAR IT.

Paper bags can come in handy in the car. Use one for a windshield cover during wintry weather. Here's how: TOTBOB and cover the windshield with the paper rectangle when your family parks the car. Then when you are ready to go, peel the sack off, along with the snow and ice. Bags can be used for floor protectors against muddy shoes. Keep one handy for a car trash bag. For a long vacation, pack paper bags with special treats and goodies for all.

10 COLLAGE IT.

TOTBOB. Cut the large rectangle into two pieces. With a friend, make collages by gluing natural things like leaves and seeds onto the paper. This is especially fun in the fall!

11 COOL IT.

Put cookies on a bag to cool after taking them off the cookie sheet.

TOTBOB—Take off the bottom, open bag.

12 CORRESPOND IT.

TOTBOB. Cut the paper up into several smaller pieces and use them to write letters on.

13 COVER IT.

TOTBOB. Cover a book with the paper. This will protect the book, and you can decorate the cover with pictures of things you like.

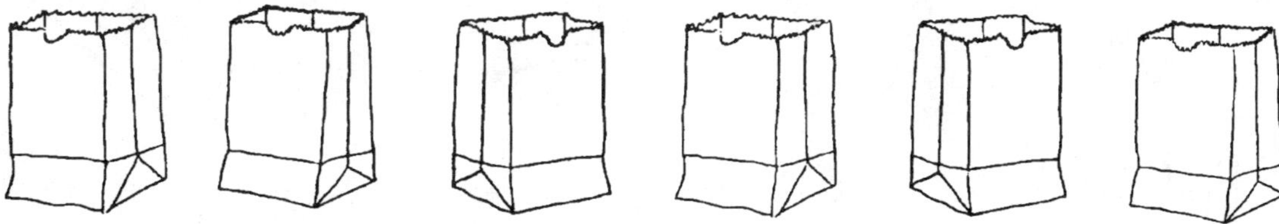

TOTBOB—Take off the bottom, open bag.

14 FEEL IT.

Make a feely bag. Fold over the top and staple it closed. Turn the bag over and gently open up one side of the bottom seam for a mouth. Round off the frown with scissors. Glue on construction paper eyes. Put wet, sticky, or other strange-feeling objects into the mouth of the feely bag. Ask friends to reach in and guess what they are feeling. (Try putting in a wet leaf, a pine cone, a gummy worm, a Koosh ball, and so forth.)

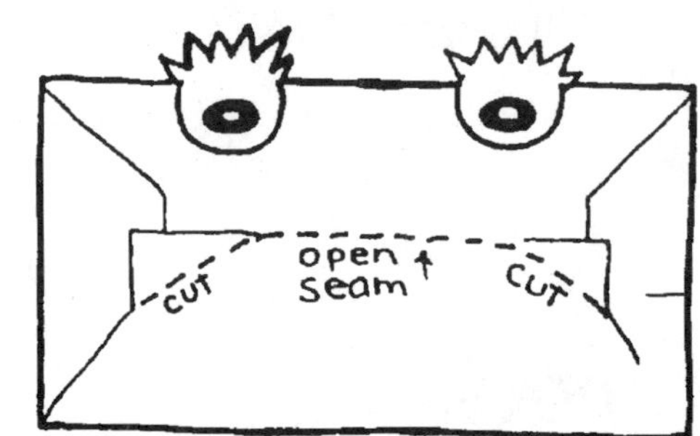

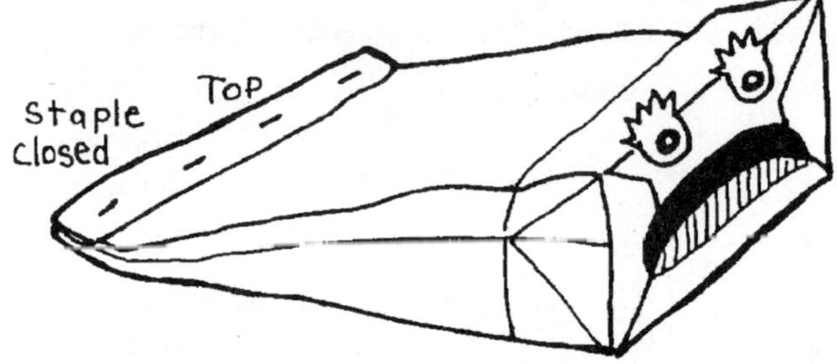

15 FILL IT.

Fill it with popcorn and bring it to a football game.

16 GINGER IT.

TOTBOB. Fold the rectangle in half, making almost a square. On one side draw a fat gingerbread boy shape. Cut it out through both bags, making two gingerbread boys. Decorate one side with features and accessories made from white paper. Paper clip the two securely together, then punch holes

TOTBOB—Take off the bottom, open bag.

around the outside edge of the gingerbread boy shapes. Lace them together with red yarn, leaving an opening on the side. Stuff with styrofoam peanuts or crumpled newspaper and then lace closed. You might make a gingerbread girl, too, and let them both sit under your Christmas tree next year.

17 HIDE IT.

Bring an item for "show and tell" to school in a bag so no one will see it early.

18 HOOP IT.

For an easy "basketball" game, put about one inch of sand in the paper bag. Set the bag at a respectable distance and practice shooting wadded-up paper "balls." For young children, paint a big clown face on the bag first.

19   LIGHT IT.

Make a set of luminaries to decorate a pathway for an evening celebration. Using smaller paper grocery bags, cut out designs on one or both sides of the bag. Try using hole punches, decorative paper punches, as well as freehand cut outs. For instance, fold the bag and make a simple snowflake design. Place one inch of sand in the bottom of each bag. Space the luminaries evenly along a sidewalk or driveway at home or church. Just before the event, place in the middle of each bag a votive candle and light it. For safety, do this project on a windless evening and extinguish the candles immediately after the event.

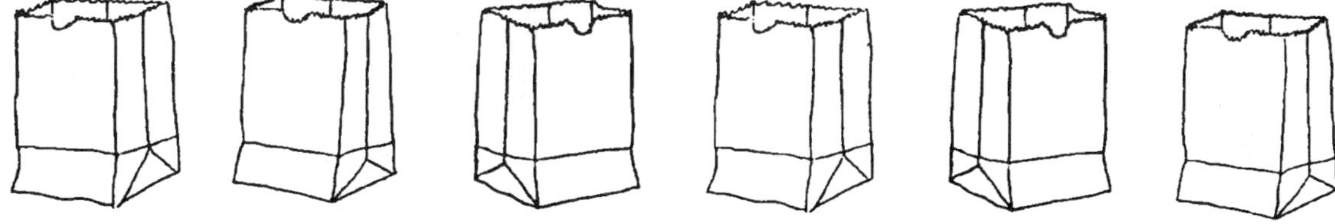

20 ORIGAMI IT.

TOTBOB, then cut two squares. Use each for an origami fold. Here's an old favorite to try: The Fortune Teller.

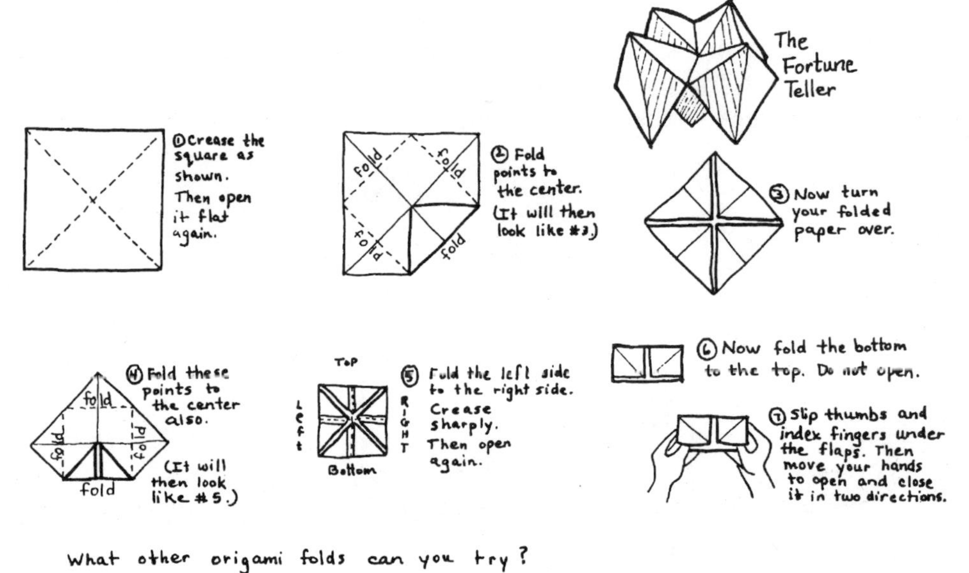

What other origami folds can you try?

TOTBOB—Take off the bottom, open bag.

21 PAINT IT.

TOTBOB. Let your imagination soar with how to cover this huge canvas. I wonder how many ways you can paint it? Here are four ideas to get you started:

Food coloring paint — Mix 1 teaspoon of water, 1 teaspoon of dish soap, and 1/2 teaspoon of food coloring. Use these bright paints to paint a picture on the bag paper.

Printing — Use interesting objects dipped in tempura paint to print designs on the paper. Try forks, cookie cutters, wood blocks, nature objects, and sponges. What else can you use?

Straw paintings — Put drops of liquid food coloring over the surface of the paper. Blow through a drinking straw close to each drop to spread the colors into spidery designs resembling a fireworks display.

String paintings — Dip strings into tempera paint and lay them on the surface of the paper. Fold the paper over on top of the string. Hold the paper down as you pull the string out. Try several different colored strings on one painting.

After displaying the painting in your family "gallery" for a while, use it for gift wrap. Or tape several paintings together for a paper tablecloth. Fold one in half, glue it closed on two sides, stuff it with styrofoam pellets, and close the remaining side to make a pillow. What else can you do with your paintings?

TOTBOB—Take off the bottom, open bag.

22 PAPER IT.

TOTBOB and use it for anything you might use a strong piece of paper for. Cut paper dolls, construct a crown, loop a chain, make a garland, or blow an elephant screecher.

For paper dolls...

fold fold fold fold

Make sure hands and feet are connected at the fold.

Can you make paper hearts or animals?

TOTBOB—Take off the bottom, open bag.

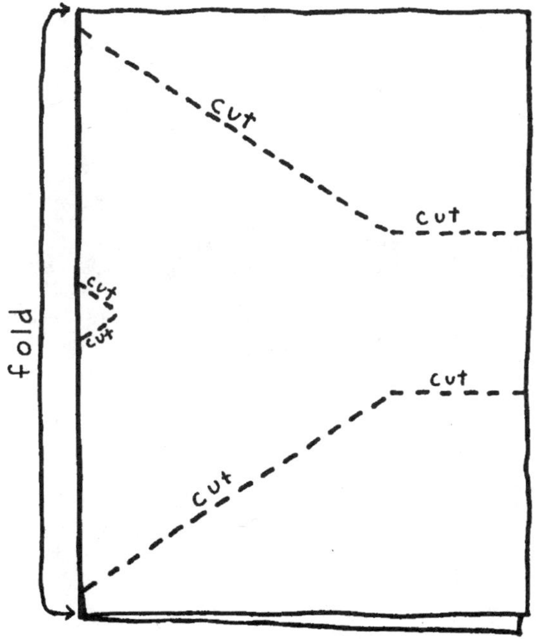

Elephant Screecher Pattern

①

②

③

④

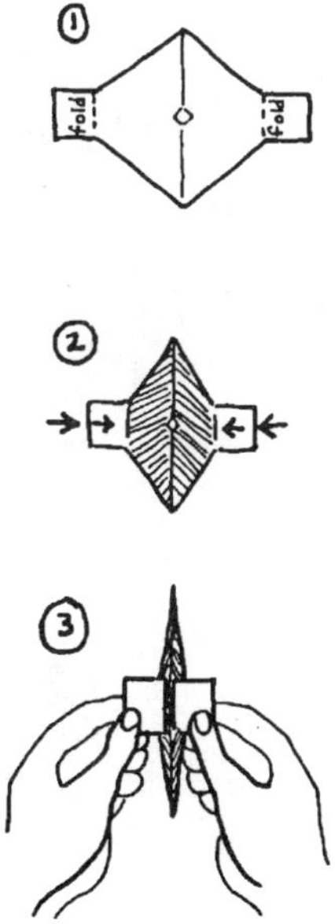

Trace the elephant screecher pattern and cut it out. Fold as shown in ① and ②. Hold as shown in ③ firmly leaving a small opening. Blow forcefully into the space as in ④. As the sides vibrate you will hear the elephant.

Make a garland for decorating at a party.

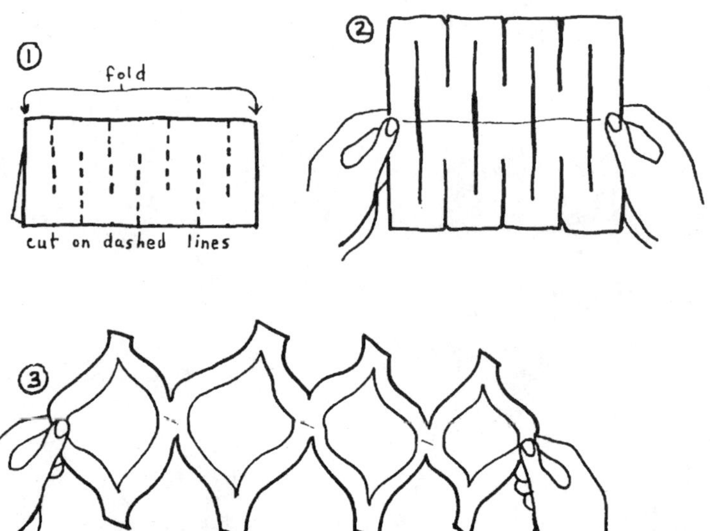

To make a twenty-foot garland, cut one ГОТ BOB in three long rectangles (about 37x6 inches). Glue them firmly together at the narrow ends, making a nine-foot strip. Color it, if you want to. Fold it in half and cut it, like in ①. Open the paper at the fold, like in ②.

Pull it apart and hang it up around the room, like in ③.

23 PAPIER MÂCHÉ IT.

TOTBOB. Cut it into two-inch squares and use with a flour and water paste to make a papier mâché statue. (Use one part flour and one part water for the paste. Thin with additional water as necessary.) If you want to build a fairly large statue, begin by building a wire foundation. Try using a balloon or crumpled paper as a foundation for smaller objects. When the statue is completely dry, paint it with tempera paints and spray it with an acrylic sealer.

24 PARADE IT.

Stuff a bag half full with crumpled newspapers. Stick an old broomstick in. Tie a string around the opening tightly, to hold the stick in the bag and to create a kind of ball on a stick. Paint a face on it, add a yarn wig, and carry it in a parade.

TOTBOB—Take off the bottom, open bag.

25 PARTY IT.

Make a piñata. Decorate a bag festively. Fill it with prizes and candies. Tie a string tightly around the top and hang it up. Take turns attempting to hit it with a stick while blindfolded. When it breaks open, everyone scrambles for the goodies.

26   PICKET IT.

Take it to the grocery store and ask the manager to try not to use so many paper bags anymore, since someone had to cut down a fifteen-year-old tree just to make enough bags for a busy store to use up in one hour. Ask the store manager to carry cloth bags that the customers might buy and re-use them.

27   PICNIC IT.

Carry a picnic lunch for four. You might want to decorate the bag first.

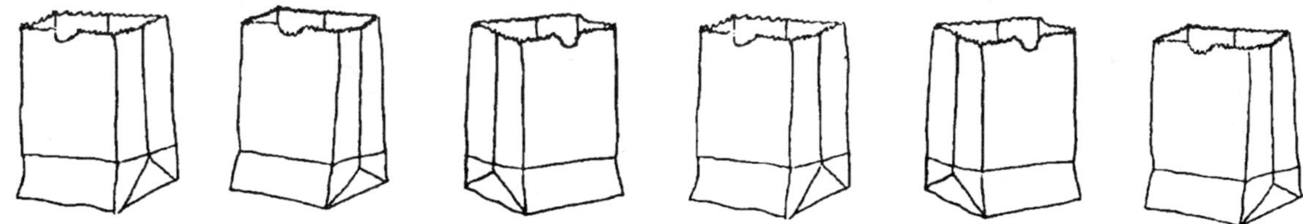

TOTBOB—Take off the bottom, open bag.

28   POP IT.

With an adult, make caramel corn. Take 1 cup brown sugar, 1 stick margarine, 1/4 cup corn syrup, and 1/2 t. salt. Combine and bring to a boil in a microwave oven. After it has come to a boil, cook on full power for two minutes. Remove and stir into it: 1/2 t. baking soda. Place four quarts of popped popcorn (be sure to remove the unpopped kernels) in a grocery bag. Pour the syrup over the popcorn, and stir with a wooden spoon. Fold over the top of the bag and place it in the microwave. Cook it on high for one-and-a-half minutes. Stir again. Then cook on high for one minute. Stir. Repeat, cooking for one additional minute, if necessary.

29   PULP IT.

To make handmade paper, tear an old bag into small pieces. Soak the pieces in lots of water overnight. Mix and mash the solution with your hands, or, for finer pulp, in the blender. Dip a sand sifter, piece of net fabric, or piece of a window screen into the solution and lift it up, draining off some of the water. Lay it on newspapers to blot more water, changing the newspapers several times. Remove the handmade paper in one piece when it is dry enough to do so. Lay it between more sheets of newspaper and roll with a rolling pin. Let it air dry.

30 QUILLERY IT.

TOTBOB. Cut the bag into one-half-inch by fourteen-inch rectangles. Roll the rectangles tightly around a pencil. Glue the paper coils onto a sheet of thin cardboard making interesting designs. (Quillery is an old-fashioned art that uses paper coils to emulate fine metal filigree work.) You might want to spray paint your quillery art work.

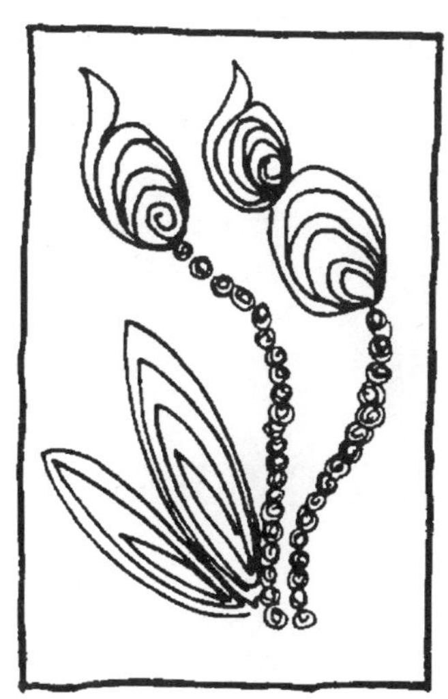

31 RACE IT.

Use paper bags for an old-fashioned sack race. Give each person in the race a large grocery bag. Everyone should stand in a straight line in a grassy area and step into their bags. On the count of three, hold onto the edge of the bag and jump carefully to the chosen finish line. The first one to cross the finish line with the bag still intact wins.

TOTBOB—Take off the bottom, open bag.

32 READ ABOUT IT.

Read <u>Benjamin Brody's Backyard Bag</u> and do some of the many things Benjamin did with his bag.

(<u>Benjamin Brody's Backyard Bag</u> was written by Phyllis Vos Wezeman and Colleen Aalsburg Wiessner and published by Brethren Press, 1451 Dundee Avenue, Elgin, Illinois, 60120, © 1991.)

33 RECOVER IT.

Make it a goal to "recover" each grocery bag you come across for the health of our earth. This can be done in many ways. Make a project in this book. When you get tired of it, recycle it with your newspapers or corrugated cardboard. You can also return bags to your grocery store and ask them to bale them for recycling with their corrugated boxes. Or fill the bag with newspapers for recycling. Or fill it with leaves and grass clippings. They will decompose together in a compost.

34 REUSE IT.

Take it back to the grocery store and have them put your groceries in it again. (Some stores will even pay you a few cents to do so.) Keep doing this until it is worn out. When it finally does wear out, buy or make a cloth bag so you can reuse it again and again for toting your groceries. (Maybe soon paper bags will be a thing of the past, and you will no longer have any use for this book!)

35 SEND IT.

TOTBOB. Wrap a package for sending in the mail. This kind of wrapping will often weigh less than a padded envelope, saving you money on postage.

36 SHAKE IT.

Make a giant maraca. Paint a bag with bright colors, if you wish. Pour in a cup or two of pebbles. Fill the rest of the bag with air. Close the top tightly using a rubber band. Shake it to the beat of lively Latin music.

TOTBOB—Take off the bottom, open bag.

37 STUFF IT.

Make creatures by using bags and parts of bags for different body parts. Stuff with crumpled newspaper. Make a jack-o-lantern or a fat scarecrow. Or make a creature from outer space. How about adding strings and sticks to make a paper bag marionette?

38 SURVEY IT.

Here is a good way to conduct a semi-confidential survey in a youth group or class. Compose four to six questions that will aid in discussing the topic for your meeting. Write one question on its own paper bag. Open the bags and display them where all can read them. Supply respondents with strips of red, yellow, and green construction paper, asking them to answer the questions using this code: red=NO, yellow=MAYBE or IT DEPENDS, and green=YES. When it is time for the discussion, you can reach in the bag and the collective opinion of the group is made clear by the colored strips.

39   TALK IT.

Make a huge hand puppet. Draw a face, making the fold into the mouth. Stick your hand in and make the puppet "talk."

40   TOSS IT.

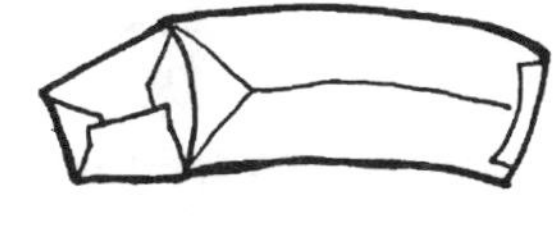

Fill one with styrofoam pellets. Slip another bag over the first all the way down to the bottom. Tape securely. Play volleyball with this rectangular prism "ball." Make a bunch of these "balls" and use them for giant-sized building blocks.

41 TRACE IT.

TOTBOB two bags. Trace around a baby lying down on the bags. (Yeah, sure! But it's worth a try. If the baby won't lie still, draw a chubby figure free-hand.) Cut out the tracing through both bags. Decorate—perhaps a construction paper face, yarn hair and fabric scrap clothes. Staple the limbs together and stuff with thin rolls of newspaper. Then continue stapling and stuffing with crushed newspaper or styrofoam pellets and staple the final opening closed. Instead of making fabric scrap clothes, you might want to dress it in one of the real baby's outfits after it is all stuffed.

TOTBOB—Take off the bottom, open bag.

42 TRASH IT.

Put a paper bag in your trash can at home to collect the trash.

43 TRICK-OR-TREAT IT.

Cut up a bag into rectangles about four inches by eight inches. Decorate the outside with Halloween pictures or stickers. Fold the rectangles in half, so they are about four inches square. Put in several coins and glue the three edges down tight. Put them in a basket and let children take one for a safe, cavity-free treat on Halloween.

44 UNLITTER IT.

Take it to the park, your school or around your home or apartment building and pick up trash that someone else left behind.

45 | WEAR IT.

AS A MASK. Try a horse head mask or an elephant mask. Or tie a string around the top, turn it over and cut the bottom off, cut out eyes and a mouth, set it on a person's head for a different sort of mask. Try a group totem pole. Give each person a one-third section of a TOTBOB. Each one makes her or his piece into a mask. Make handles for the masks using the bottom of the bag. Play a lively native dance tune and you and your friends can move with your masks. Then hang them on the wall together in totem pole fashion. What other kinds of masks can you make?

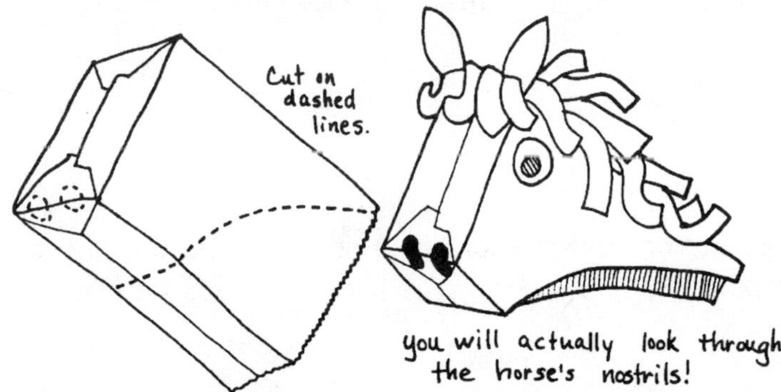

TOTBOB—Take off the bottom, open bag.

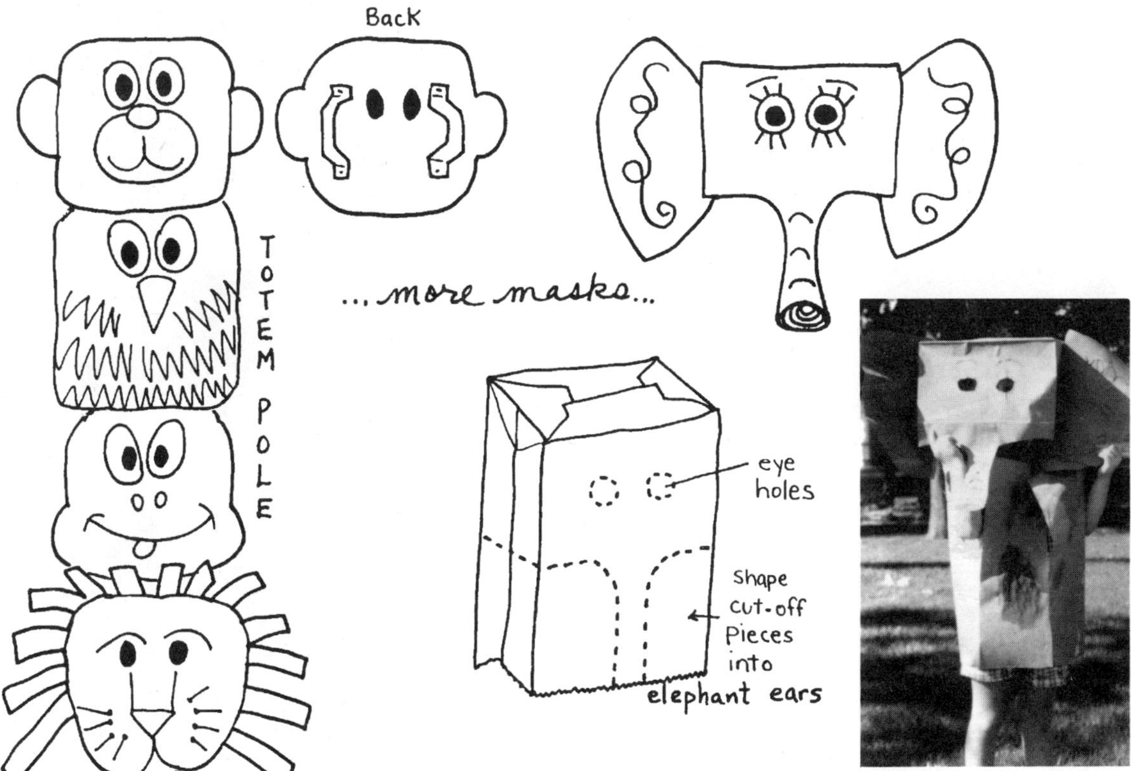
Back
...more masks...
TOTEM POLE
eye holes
Shape cut-off pieces into elephant ears

AS A SKIRT. Make a skirt for dressing up. Take the bottom off a bag. Fold the top over into the bag about an inch, then punch holes through the doubled waist band and lace it with a cord. Decorate the skirt by painting it or by gluing on brightly colored ribbons, fabric scraps, bows and buttons. Gather it around your waist and use the cord to tie a bow.

AS A VEST. Cut out a space for the head and arm holes. Then use your imagination to transform the paper bag into a creature, hero, robot or whatever. Glue feather-shaped pieces of construction paper all over the vest to be a fine-feathered friend—perhaps Big Bird. What else can you do with a vest?

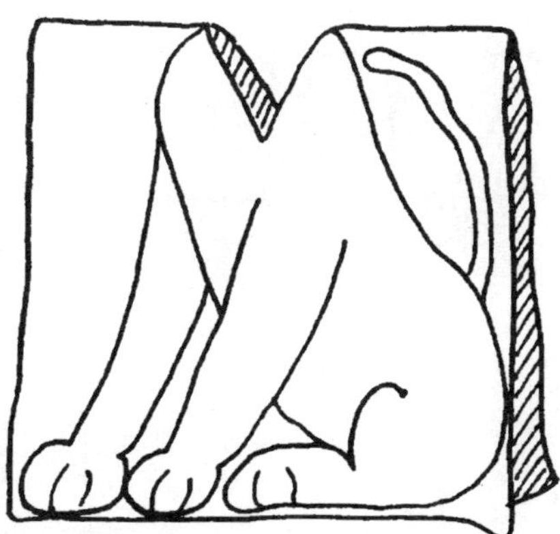

Make a poncho. Fold a TOTBOB in half. Cut a neck hole out of the middle. Paint a design on it and wear it for a costume.

AS A WIG. Cut out a rectangle big enough for a face to fit through. Cut the sides of the bag into long skinny strips. For curly hair roll the strips around a pencil. Tie a scarf around the top and under the chin to hold it onto the head of the wearer. Or fit a hat on top of the wig. The hair will hang out all around.

46 WEAVE IT.

Instead of the popular woven fabric and paper twist basket, make your woven basket with all paper bag strips. Paint it to suit your taste. Or for a simple basket, take one bag and fold the top half inward, toward the bottom of the bag, to make a half-bag. Add glue into the folded area. Turn it over onto its top while it dries so the glue doesn't drip onto the bottom of the bag. Spray paint it. Make a bunch of them for storing lightweight objects on your craft or toy shelf.

47 WEED IT.

Give one to each member in your family. See who can fill theirs with the most weeds from your yard and garden. After the contest, empty the bags into a compost pile and re-use the bags on another gardening day. When they get really old and dirty throw them into the compost pile, too. They will decompose.

Here's a simple way to make a compost pile if you don't already have one: With chicken wire fencing make a circle that measures about four feet across and is two feet tall. Dump in organic waste from the kitchen and yard. "Organic" is stuff that was once living, like grass clippings, fruit and vegetable peels, corn cobs, leaves, and weeds. (One exception: don't put in meat, bones, or fat.) Turn the compost pile over with a pitch fork every two or three weeks and watch it turn into rich soil that you can return to your garden.

48 WRAP IT.

TOTBOB. Cover the sheet of grocery bag paper with colorful hand prints using tempura paints. This will make a treasured sheet of wrapping paper for a Fathers' Day or Mothers' Day gift.

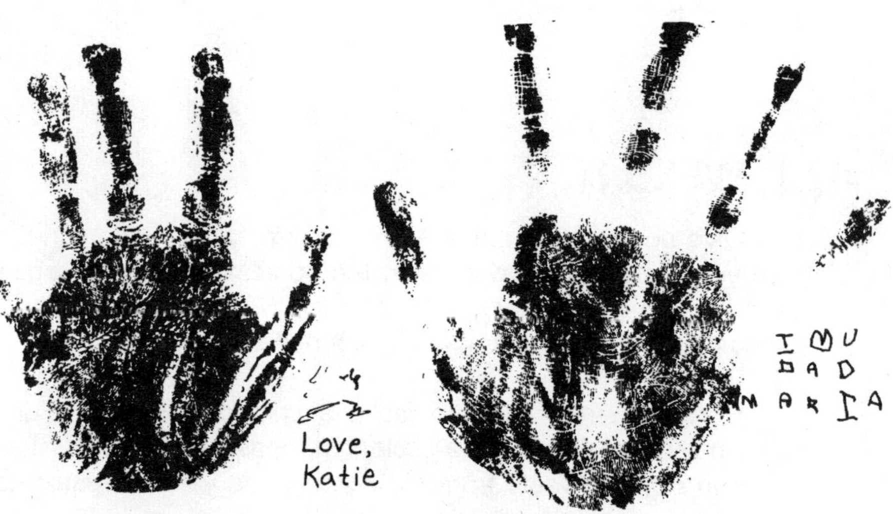

TOTBOB—Take off the bottom, open bag.

49 WREATH IT.

TOTBOB. Cut the bag lengthwise into three strips. (They will each be about six inches by thirty-seven inches long.) Roll each into a long loose roll. Glue the three ends together and secure with a clothespin. Braid the paper rolls. (It works best if one person holds the end while a second person braids it.) When finished, form the braid into a circle, weaving the three loose ends into the wreath, as best you can. Glue the ends together. Decorate with flowers, ribbons, and a bow. (Place the bow over the seam to hide the irregular place in the area where it was glued.) Add a loop of yarn and hang it up.

TOTBOB—Take off the bottom, open bag.

50 WRITE IT.

Write a long list on one. How about a list of all the things <u>you</u> might do with a paper grocery bag? Begin your list with #51.

PAPER VS. PLASTIC GROCERY BAGS

Which is better for the environment—paper or plastic grocery bags? There is no simple answer to that question. Here are some of the good things about each type of bag.

❖ Paper bags are made from wood and wood is a renewable resource. New trees are being planted as others are cut down.

❖ Paper bags are biodegradable when composted. Within seven days they can "return to the earth." Although nothing—not paper, plastic, or even food wastes—can degrade within modern, U.S. landfills, many communities are beginning composting programs where paper grocery bags could be composted. Also, for those grocery bags that unfortunately end up as litter, paper bags degrade easily and don't remain on land and sea as a nuisance and as a danger to wildlife.

❖ Paper bags are recyclable—in fact, paper bag fibers are valuable and versatile in the recycling process because of their strength.

❖ Paper bags use post-consumer waste. Many paper bags are made partly from recycled newspaper and corrugated cardboard. Today, paper grocery bags have an average of 25 percent recovered paper fibers in them.

❖ Paper bags are reusable for toting groceries and other things. They are also fun to use for making nifty things.

❖ Paper bags are rugged and durable, and they stand up with groceries in them.

❖ Paper bags are endorsed by Responsible Environmental Action Programs (REAP).

❖ A large paper grocery bag holds 30 to 50 percent more than a plastic bag of a comparable size.

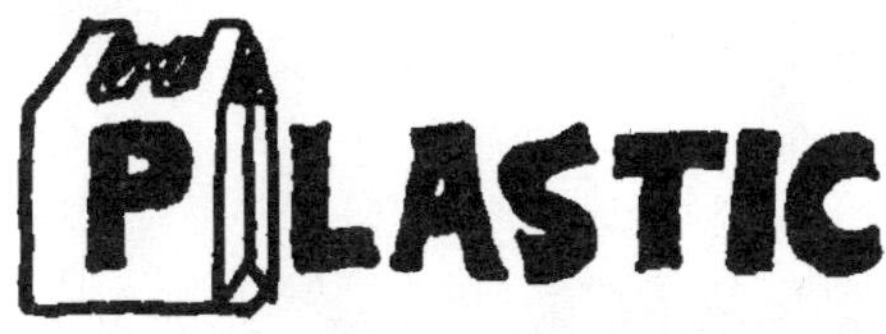

PLASTIC

❖ An environmental impact study, done by Franklin Associates, Ltd. in 1990, concluded that plastic grocery bags consume 40 percent less energy, and create 80 percent less solid waste and at least 70 percent less air and water pollution throughout their lifecycles than paper grocery bags.

❖ Plastic grocery bags take up one-seventh the space of an equal number of paper grocery bags—this saves fuel since it would take seven trucks to ship the same number of paper grocery bags as one truckload of plastic grocery bags. Plastic grocery bags also save more space in landfills when disposed of.

❖ Convenient carrying handles mean that you can carry more groceries in one hand with plastic bags.

❖ Plastic bags are waterproof and reusable for storage, trash can liners, totes, and many other things that help extend their life.

❖ Plastic bags cost less for supermarkets to purchase.

❖ Plastic bags are recyclable. They are made into things like plastic envelopes, plastic lumber, drain pipes and new plastic bags.

CLOTH BAGGING IS THE BEST ENVIRONMENTAL CHOICE.

❖ According to the EPA, the most important priority for the future of waste management is source reduction. **Of the Three R's—Reduce, Reuse, Recycle—reducing is going to make the greatest difference for our environment.** If we reduce our need for disposable grocery bags, less energy and resources will be used in producing the packaging and, consequently, waste and pollution will be reduced. Please try to reduce the need for plastic and paper grocery bags by bringing your own cloth bags to the grocery store.

Here are some organizations you can write or call to get information and to tell them your concerns. These groups are listening to your call to care for the earth.

Plastic Bag Information Clearinghouse
1817 E. Carson Street
Pittsburgh, PA 15203
1-800-438-5856

The American Plastics Council (APC)
1275 K Street, N.W., Suite 400
Washington, D.C. 20005
1-800-777-9500

The Paper Bag Institute, Inc.
505 White Plains Road.
Tarrytown, NY 10591
1 -914-631-0696

American Forest and
   Paper Association
260 Madison Avenue
New York, NY 10016
1-800-878-8878